I0435116

United States
Department of
Agriculture

Forest Service

**Southern
Research Station**

Resource Bulletin
SRS–154

# Kentucky's Timber Industry–
# An Assessment of Timber Product
# Output and Use, 2007

Rhonda M. Mathison
and Christopher G. Nevins

## The Authors:

**Rhonda M. Mathison**, Forester, U.S. Forest Service, Southern Research Station, Knoxville, TN 37919; **Christopher G. Nevins**, Forester, Kentucky Division of Forestry, Frankfort, KY 40601.

June 2009

Southern Research Station
200 W.T. Weaver Blvd.
Asheville, NC 28804

## Foreword

This report contains the findings of a 2007 canvass of all primary wood-using plants in Kentucky, and presents changes in product output and residue use since 2005. It complements the Forest Inventory and Analysis periodic inventory of volume and removals from the State's timberland. The canvass was conducted to determine the amount and source of wood receipts and annual timber product drain, by county, in 2007 and to determine interstate and cross-regional movement of industrial roundwood. Only primary wood-using mills were canvassed. Primary mills are those that process roundwood in log or bolt form or as chipped roundwood. Examples of industrial roundwood products are saw logs, pulpwood, veneer logs, poles, and logs used for composite board products. Mills producing products from residues generated at primary and secondary processors were not canvassed. Trees chipped in the woods were included in the estimate of timber drain only if they were delivered to a primary domestic manufacturer.

A 100-percent canvass of certain wood processors in Kentucky was conducted in 2008 to obtain information for 2007. In addition, roundwood from out-of-State mills known to be using logs or bolts harvested from Kentucky timberland was incorporated into Kentucky production estimates. Each mill was canvassed by mail or through personal contact at plant locations. Telephone contacts followed mailed questionnaire responses when additional information or clarification of a response was necessary.

In the event of a nonresponse, data collected in previous surveys were updated using current data collected for mills of similar size, product type, and location. Surveys for all timber products other than pulpwood began in 1948, and are currently conducted every 2 years.

Pulpwood production data were taken from an annual canvass of all southern pulpmills. Medium density fiberboard, insulating board, and hardboard plants were included in this survey.

## Acknowledgments

The authors thank Larry Lowe and Amos Stone for review and comments; Carolyn Steppleton, Michael Howell and James Bentley for their tireless efforts in processing and accuracy of the data; Helen Beresford for timber product output database maintenance and support; Anne Jenkins, Janet Griffin, Sharon Johnson, and Charlene Walker for tables, graphs, and statistical checking; and the Southern Research Station (SRS) Technical Publications Team for editorial review, styling, and publication of this report.

The SRS gratefully acknowledges the cooperation and assistance provided by the Kentucky Division of Forestry in collecting mill data. Appreciation is also extended to forest industry and mill managers for providing timber products information.

## Timber Product Output Database Retrieval System

The Forest Inventory and Analysis (FIA) Research Work Unit of the USDA Forest Service developed the Timber Product Output (TPO) Database Retrieval System to help customers answer questions about timber harvesting and use in the Southern Region. This system acts as an interface to a standard set of consistently coded TPO data for each State and county in the region and Nation. This regional and national set of TPO data consists of 11 variables that describe for each county the roundwood products harvested, logging residues left in the woods, other timber removals (i.e. land clearing and reserved timber removals), and wood and bark residues generated by the county's primary wood-using mills. The system is available through the FIA Web site: http://srsfia2.fs.fed.us/.

The database is well documented and easy to use. The retrieval system allows the user to select the TPO variables of interest and generate a standard set of timber products, removals, and mill residue tables for the specified resource area, State, or region. The system has been logically divided into two sections to assist the user in making specific data requests. In section 1, the user is asked to define the resource area, and section 2 generates tables for the specified area. In each section, the user is asked to supply specific options that will serve to customize the database retrieval.

There are four options available for defining the geographic area of interest. Each option provides an increasing level of detail. The region, subregion, State, or county defines an area. The user selects the option that best suits the level of detail required. Users who select county as an option should be aware that some counties have been combined due to data sensitivity. These combined counties are identified with asterisks in the output tables.

The TPO contacts are listed for each region to provide additional explanation or clarification.

Tony Johnson
Southern Research Station
USDA Forest Service
4700 Old Kingston Pike
Knoxville, TN 37919
tjohnson09@fs.fed.us
865-862-2042

Helen Beresford
Southern Research Station
USDA Forest Service
4700 Old Kingston Pike
Knoxville, TN 37919
hberesford@fs.fed.us
865-862-2091

James Bentley
Southern Research Station
USDA Forest Service
4700 Old Kingston Pike
Knoxville, TN 37919
jbentley@fs.fed.us
865-862-2056

Carolyn Steppleton
Southern Research Station
USDA Forest Service
200 W.T. Weaver Blvd.
Asheville, NC 28804
csteppleton@fs.fed.us
828-257-4848

# Contents

[a] All tables in this report are available in Microsoft® Excel workbook files. Upon request, these files will be supplied in the format the customer requests.

The use of trade or firm names in this publication is for reader information and does not imply endorsement by the U.S. Department of Agriculture of any product or service.

**Production** = Retained + Exports          **Receipts** = Retained + Imports

Figure 1—Movement of roundwood exports and imports within the United States.

# Kentucky's Timber Industry— An Assessment of Timber Product Output and Use, 2007

**Rhonda M. Mathison and Christopher G. Nevins**

## Output of Industrial Timber Products

Note: Certain terms used in this report—retained, export, import, production, and receipts—have specialized meanings unique to Forest Inventory and Analysis Units across the country that deal with timber product output (TPO) (fig. 1).

## All Products

- Between 2005 and 2007, TPO from roundwood was down 5.5 million cubic feet, or 3 percent, to 186 million cubic feet, while output of utilized plant byproducts decreased 2.8 million cubic feet to 88 million cubic feet.

- Output of hardwood roundwood products decreased 3 percent to 174 million cubic feet, while output of softwood roundwood products was down 8 percent to 12 million cubic feet (fig. 2).

- Saw logs and pulpwood were the principal roundwood products in 2007. Combined output of these products totaled 169 million cubic feet and accounted for 91 percent of Kentucky's total roundwood output (fig. 3).

- Total receipts at Kentucky mills, which included roundwood harvested and retained in the State, as well as roundwood imported from other States, declined 7 percent to 200 million cubic feet. At the same time, the number of primary roundwood-using plants in Kentucky declined from 292 in 2005 to 253 in 2007 (fig. 4).

- Across all products, 85 percent of roundwood harvested was retained for processing at Kentucky mills. Exports of roundwood to other States amounted to 29 million cubic feet, while imports of roundwood amounted to 43 million cubic feet, making the State a net importer of roundwood. Tables A.8 to A.11 show exports to and imports from other States by individual product type.

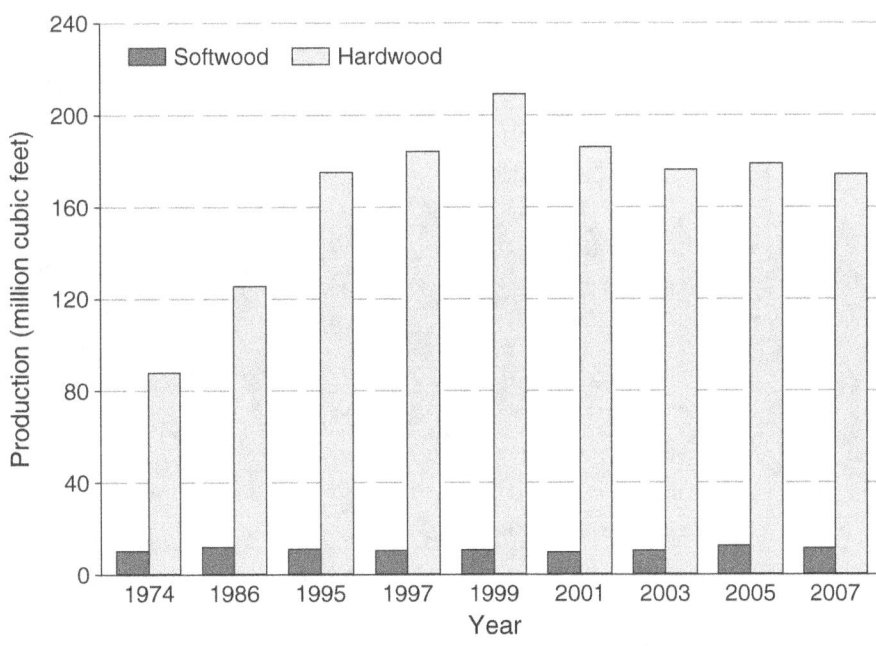

Figure 2—Roundwood production for all products by species group and year (see page 7 for references for individual years), Kentucky.

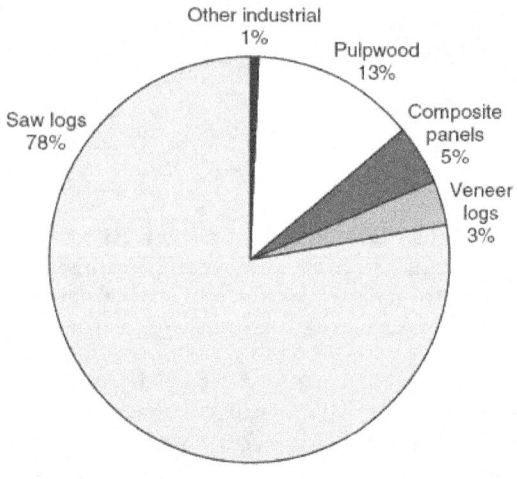

Total 186 million cubic feet

Figure 3—Roundwood production by type of product, Kentucky, 2007.

## Saw Logs

- Saw logs accounted for 78 percent of the State's total roundwood products. Output of hardwood saw logs increased 1 percent to 140 million cubic feet (856 million board feet, International ¼-inch rule), while that of softwood saw logs decreased 6 percent to 4.2 million cubic feet (23 million board feet, International ¼-inch rule) (fig. 5).

- In 2007, Kentucky had 241 sawmills, a net loss of 36 mills since 2005. Total saw-log receipts were down 5 million cubic feet to 140 million cubic feet. Hardwood saw-log receipts decreased by 3 percent to 136 million cubic feet, while those of softwoods increased 1 percent to 4 million cubic feet. Of the operating mills, 39 percent had receipts of <1 million board feet, 42 percent had receipts of between 1 and 4.99 million board feet, while 19 percent had receipts of 5 million board feet or greater. Those 46 mills accounted for 63 percent of total saw-log receipts.

- Kentucky retained 91 percent of its saw-log production for manufacture in State; saw-log exports exceeded imports by 4 million cubic feet in 2007.

## Pulpwood

- Total pulpwood production, including chipped round-wood, increased 56,000 cubic feet to 25 million cubic feet and accounted for 13 percent of the State's total roundwood TPO. Hardwood output remained stable at 20 million cubic feet (268,000 cords); softwood output remained stable at 4 million cubic feet (57,000 cords) (fig. 6).

Primary wood-using mills

- • Sawmill (0–5 mmbf)   ▲ Composite panel   ☆ Other
- ● Sawmill (5–20 mmbf)   ✚ Veneer
- ⬤ Sawmill (> 20 mmbf)   ■ Pulpmill

Figure 4—Primary wood-using mills by region, Kentucky, 2007.

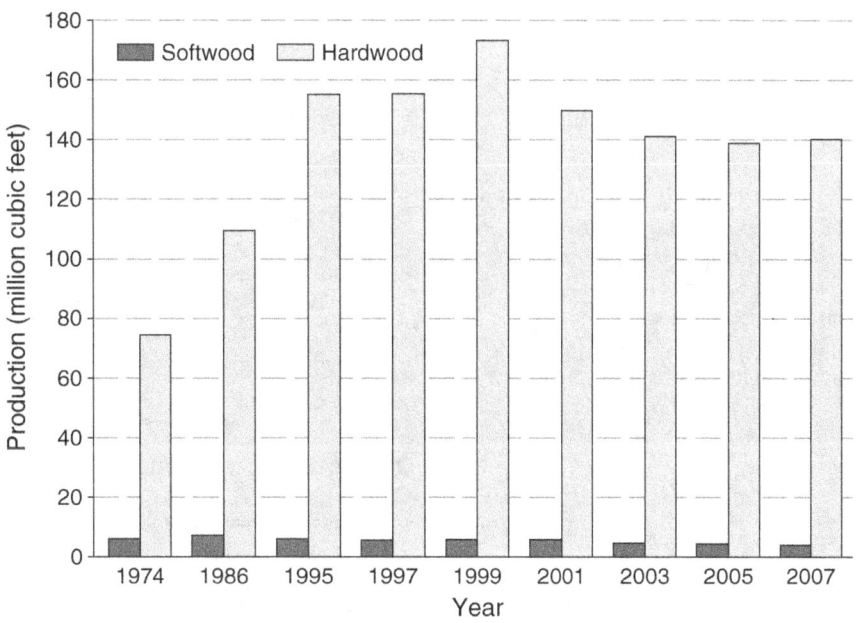

Figure 5—Roundwood saw-log production by species group and year (see page 7 for references for individual years), Kentucky.

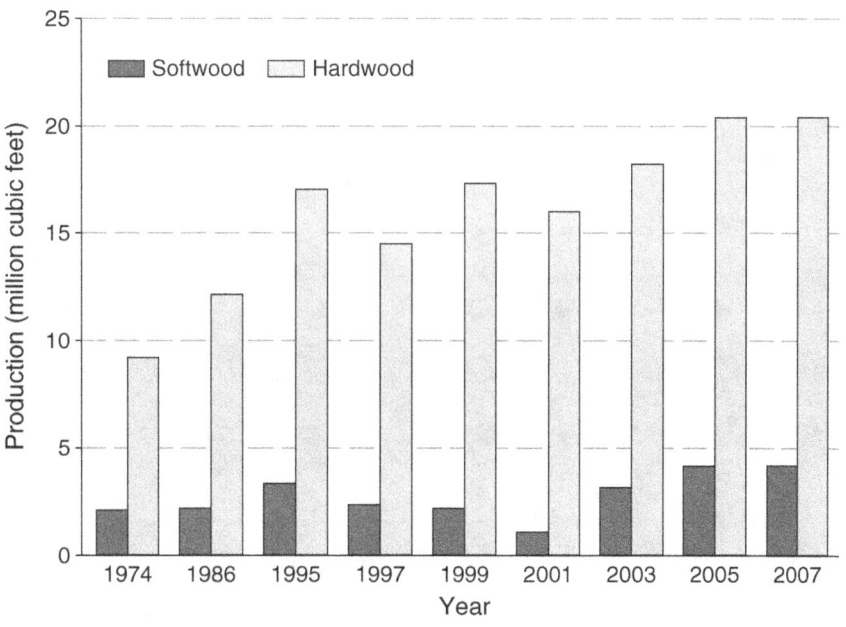

Figure 6—Roundwood pulpwood production by species group and year (see page 7 for references for individual years), Kentucky.

- Two pulpmill facilities were operating and receiving roundwood in Kentucky in 2007, the same as in 2005. Total pulpwood receipts for these mills declined 8 percent, or 4.3 million cubic feet, to 51 million cubic feet, accounting for 26 percent of total receipts for all mills.

- Seventy-four percent of roundwood cut for pulpwood was retained for processing at Kentucky pulpmills. Roundwood pulpwood accounted for 22 percent of total known exports and 77 percent of total imports. Roundwood pulpwood imports amounted to 33 million cubic feet, while exports amounted to 6 million cubic feet, making the State a net importer of pulpwood.

## Veneer Logs

- Output of veneer logs was down 13 percent in 2007 and totaled 6.5 million cubic feet (41 million board feet, International ¼-inch rule), 99 percent of which was hardwood (fig. 7). Veneer-log production accounted for 3 percent of the State's total roundwood TPO volume.

- Three veneer mills operated in Kentucky in 2007. Total receipts of veneer logs decreased 23 percent to 1.5 million cubic feet.

- Kentucky retained 7 percent of its veneer-log production for processing within the State. Imports amounted to 1 million cubic feet, and exports totaled 6 million cubic feet, making the State a net exporter of roundwood veneer logs.

## Composite Panels

- Roundwood harvested from Kentucky's forests for composite panels declined 37 percent to 9 million cubic feet (118,000 cords). Hardwood output accounted for the majority of composite panel production in Kentucky (fig. 8).

## Other Industrial Products

- Roundwood harvested for other industrial uses, such as poles, posts, mulch, firewood, and all other industrial products, totaled 1.3 million cubic feet and accounted for <1 percent of the State's total TPO. Softwood made up all of the other industrial product volume.

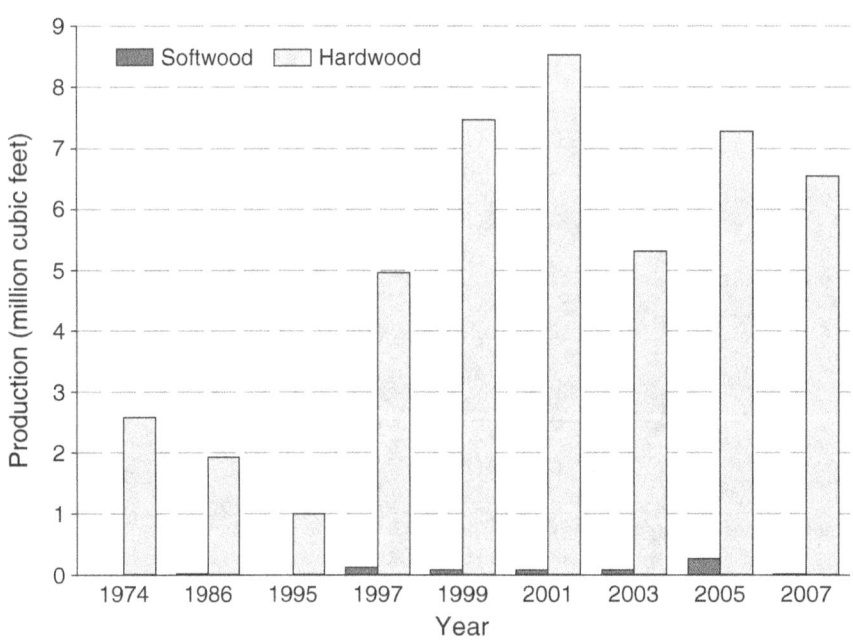

Figure 7—Roundwood veneer-log production by species group and year (see page 7 for references for individual years), Kentucky.

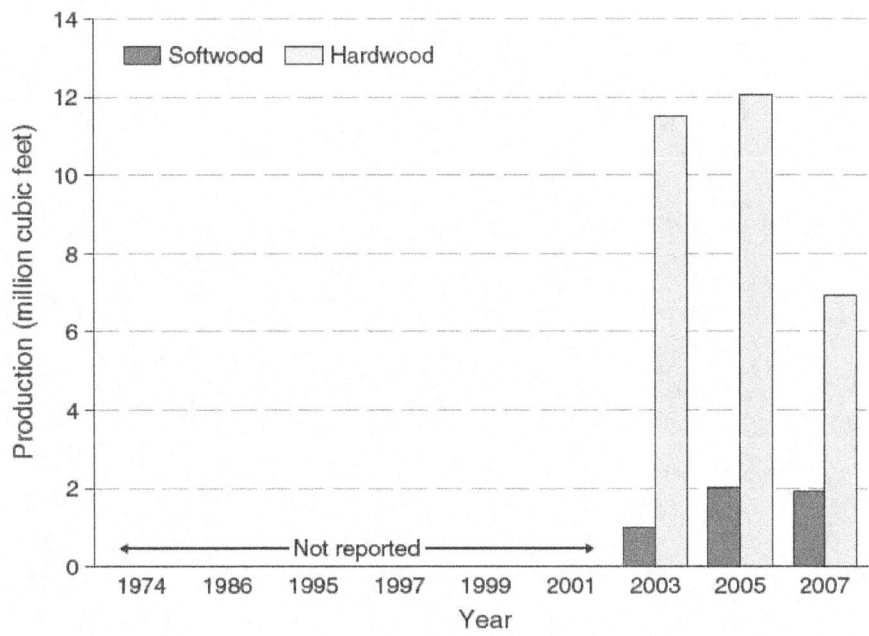

Figure 8—Roundwood production for composite panels by species group and year (see page 7 for references for individual years), Kentucky.

## Plant Byproducts

- In 2007, processing of primary products in Kentucky mills generated 90 million cubic feet of wood and bark residues. Coarse residues from all primary products amounted to 39 million cubic feet, and bark volume totaled 22 million cubic feet. Sawdust and shavings made up 32 percent of total residues, or 29 million cubic feet (fig. 9).

- The processing of saw logs at sawmills generated 81 million cubic feet of mill residues, accounting for 90 percent of the total residues produced (fig. 10).

- Ninety-eight percent of the wood and bark residues were used for a product, with 31 percent of the residues used for fuel (fig. 11). Twenty million cubic feet, or 51 percent, of the coarse residues were used to manufacture fiber products. Most of the bark was used for other miscellaneous products or industrial fuel, and 53 percent of the sawdust and shavings were used for fuel.

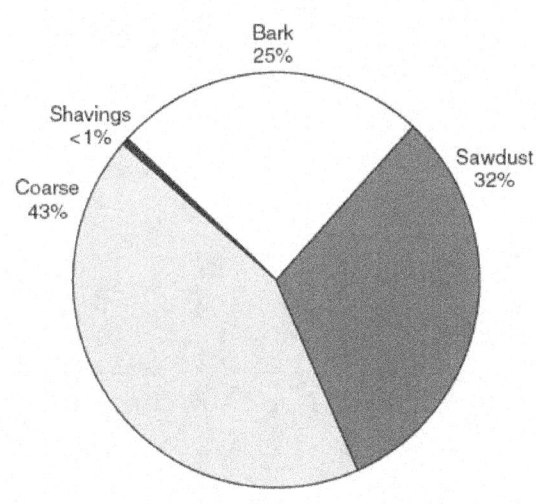

Total 90 million cubic feet

Figure 9—Primary mill residue by residue type, Kentucky, 2007.

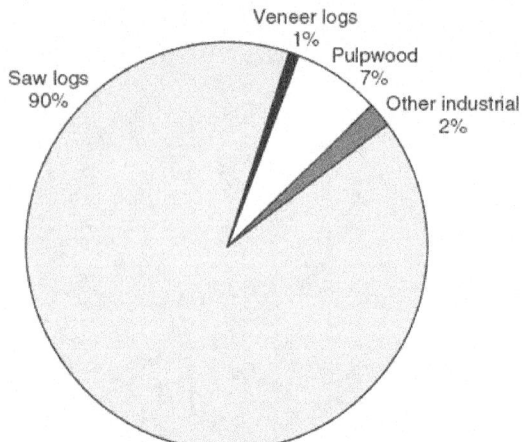

Total 90 million cubic feet

Figure 10—Primary mill residue produced by roundwood type, Kentucky, 2007.

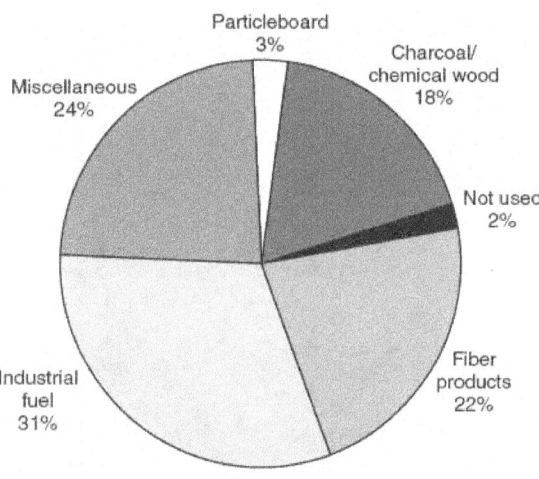

Total 90 million cubic feet

Figure 11—Disposal of residue by product, Kentucky, 2007.

## County Data

- Table A.14 shows softwood and hardwood product output by county and individual product type. All 120 counties in Kentucky had either or both softwood and hardwood output. Five counties (Greenup, Knox, Laurel, Lewis, and Ohio) had combined softwood and hardwood product output of > 5 million cubic feet each. These five counties' total product output amounted to nearly 35 million cubic feet and accounted for 19 percent of the State's total product output.

## Total Roundwood Output

Using the most recent inventory data for Kentucky, product output by source, ownership, and detailed species group was estimated.

### Source

- In addition to the 186 million cubic feet of roundwood output for industrial roundwood, an estimated 21 million cubic feet were harvested for domestic fuelwood, bringing Kentucky's total roundwood output to 206 million cubic feet.

- Eighty-eight percent of total roundwood output was considered growing-stock volume (sawtimber and poletimber) from timberland sources. Other sources (such as saplings; stumps, tops, and limbs of trees on timberland; and trees on nonforest land) contributed an estimated 25 million cubic feet, or 12 percent of total roundwood output (fig. 12).

### Ownership

- An estimated 197 million cubic feet, or 95 percent, of the total roundwood output in 2007 came from nonindustrial private forest lands. Forest industry lands contributed 7 million cubic feet, or 3 percent of the output. Public lands made up the remaining 2 percent, or 3.2 million cubic feet (fig. 13).

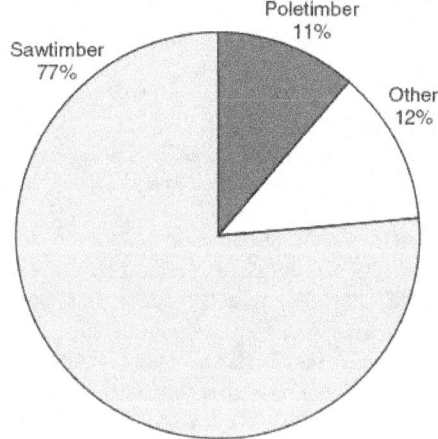

Total 206 million cubic feet

Figure 12—Roundwood output by source, Kentucky, 2007.

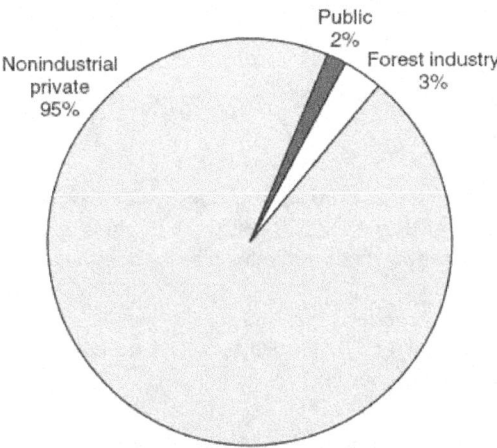

Figure 13—Roundwood output by ownership, Kentucky, 2007.

Total 206 million cubic feet

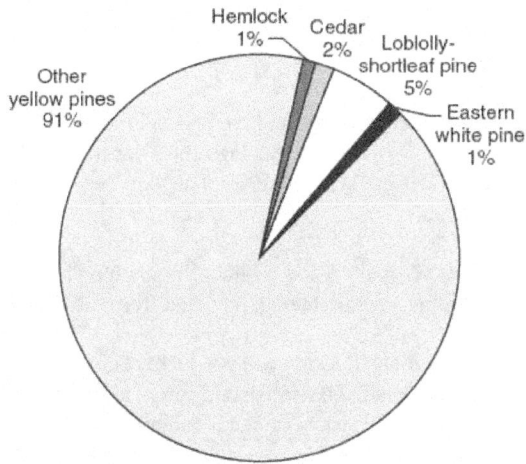

Total 12 million cubic feet

Figure 15—Roundwood output by softwood species group, Kentucky, 2007.

## Species

- The red oak and white oak groups combined accounted for 94 million cubic feet, or 49 percent of total hardwood output (fig. 14). Yellow-poplar and hickory accounted for 14 and 11 percent, respectively, of the total hardwood output. Other yellow pines provided more volume than any other softwood species group, accounting for 91 percent of the total softwood output (fig. 15). The loblolly and shortleaf pine types accounted for 5 percent of the softwood output.

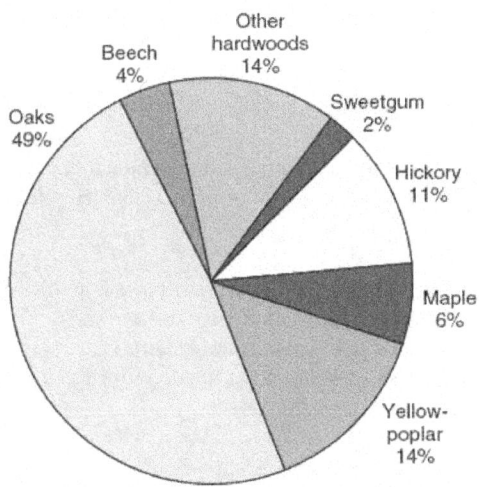

Total 195 million cubic feet

Figure 14—Roundwood output by hardwood species group, Kentucky, 2007.

## References

Alerich, C.L. 1990. Forest statistics for Kentucky—1975 and 1988. Resour. Bull. NE–117. Radnor, PA: U.S. Department of Agriculture Forest Service, Northeastern Forest Experiment Station. 295 p. [1986].

Bentley, J.W.; Lowe, L. 2004. Kentucky's timber industry—an assessment of timber product output and use, 2001. Resour. Bull. SRS–90. Asheville, NC: U.S. Department of Agriculture Forest Service, Southern Research Station. 45 p. [2001].

Bentley, J.W.; Lowe, L. 2006. Kentucky's timber industry—an assessment of timber product output and use, 2003. Resour. Bull. SRS–105. Asheville, NC: U.S. Department of Agriculture Forest Service, Southern Research Station. 50 p. [2003].

Bentley, J.W.; Lowe, L. 2007. Kentucky's timber industry—an assessment of timber product output and use, 2005. Resour. Bull. SRS–124. Asheville, NC: U.S. Department of Agriculture Forest Service, Southern Research Station. 32 p. [2005].

Bones, J.T.; Lohr, C.J. 1977. The timber industries of Kentucky. Resour. Bull. NE–50. Upper Darby, PA: U.S. Department of Agriculture Forest Service, Northeastern Forest Experiment Station. 26 p. [1974].

Johnson, T.G.; Jenkins, A.; Lowe, L. 1997. Kentucky's timber industry—an assessment of timber product output and use, 1995. Resour. Bull. SRS–20. Asheville, NC: U.S. Department of Agriculture Forest Service, Southern Research Station. 33 p. [1995].

Johnson, T.G.; Lowe, L. 2002. Kentucky's timber industry—an assessment of timber product output and use, 1999. Resour. Bull. SRS–71. Asheville, NC: U.S. Department of Agriculture Forest Service, Southern Research Station. 45 p. [1999].

Little, E.L., Jr. 1979. Checklist of United States trees (native and naturalized). Agric. Handb. 541. Washington, DC: U.S. Department of Agriculture. 375 p.

Stratton, D.; Lowe, L. 1999. Kentucky's timber industry—an assessment of timber product output and use, 1997. Resour. Bull. SRS–40. Asheville, NC: U.S. Department of Agriculture Forest Service, Southern Research Station. 40 p. [1997].

# Glossary

**Board foot.** A unit of measure applied to lumber that is 1-foot long, 1-foot wide, and 1-inch thick (or its equivalent) and also associated with roundwood as to its potential yield of such products.

**Byproducts.** Primary wood products, e.g., pulp chips, animal bedding, and fuelwood, recycled from mill residues.

**Composite panels.** Roundwood products manufactured into chips, wafers, strands, flakes, shavings, or sawdust and then reconstituted into a variety of panel and engineered lumber products.

**Consumption.** The quantity of a commodity, such as pulpwood, utilized by a particular mill or group of mills.

**Domestic fuelwood.** The volume of roundwood harvested to produce heat for residential settings.

**Drain.** The volume of roundwood removed from any geographic area where timber is grown.

**Exports.** The volume of domestic roundwood utilized by mills outside the State where timber was cut.

**Fiber products.** Byproducts used in the manufacture of pulp, paper, paperboard, and composite products, such as chipboard.

**Growing-stock removals.** The growing-stock volume removed from poletimber and sawtimber trees in the timberland inventory. (Note: Includes volume removed for roundwood products, logging residues, and other removals.)

**Growing-stock trees.** Living trees of commercial species classified as sawtimber, poletimber, saplings, and seedlings. Growing-stock trees must contain at least one 12-foot or two 8-foot logs in the saw-log portion, currently or potentially (if too small to qualify). The log(s) must meet dimension and merchantability standards and have, currently or potentially, one-third of the gross board-foot volume in sound wood.

**Growing-stock volume.** The cubic-foot volume of sound wood in growing-stock trees at least 5.0 inches d.b.h. from a 1-foot stump to a minimum 4.0-inch top d.o.b. of the central stem.

**Hardwoods.** Dicotyledonous trees, usually broadleaf and deciduous.

*Soft hardwoods.* Hardwood species with an average specific gravity of 0.50 or less, such as gums, yellow-poplar, cottonwoods, red maple, basswoods, and willows.

*Hard hardwoods.* Hardwood species with an average specific gravity > 0.50, such as oaks, hard maples, hickories, and beech.

**Imports.** The volume of domestic roundwood delivered to a mill or group of mills in a specific State but harvested outside that State.

**Industrial fuelwood.** A roundwood product, with or without bark, used to generate energy at a manufacturing facility such as a wood-using mill.

**Industrial roundwood products.** Any primary use of the main stem of a tree, such as saw logs, pulpwood, veneer logs, intended to be processed into primary wood products such as lumber, wood pulp, sheathing, at primary wood-using mills.

**International ¼-inch rule.** A log rule or formula for estimating the board-foot volume of logs, allowing ½-inch of taper for each 4-foot length. The rule appears in a number of forms that allow for kerf. In the form used by FIA, a ¼-inch of kerf is assumed. This rule is used as the USDA Forest Service standard log rule in the Eastern United States.

**Log.** A primary forest product harvested in long, primarily 8-, 12-, and 16-foot lengths.

**Logging residues.** The unused merchantable portion of growing-stock trees cut or destroyed during logging operations.

**Merchantable portion.** That portion of live trees 5.0 inches d.b.h. and larger between a 1-foot stump and a minimum 4.0-inch top d.o.b. on the central stem. That portion of primary forks from the point of occurrence to a minimum 4.0-inch top d.o.b. is included.

**Merchantable volume.** Solid-wood volume in the merchantable portion of live trees.

**Noncommercial species.** Tree species of typically small size, poor form, or inferior quality that normally do not develop into trees suitable for industrial wood products.

**Nonforest land.** Land that has never supported forests and land formerly forested where timber production is precluded by development for other uses.

**Nongrowing-stock sources.** The net volume removed from the nongrowing-stock portions of poletimber and sawtimber trees (stumps, tops, limbs, cull sections of central stem) and from any portion of a rough, rotten, sapling, dead, or nonforest tree.

**Other forest land.** Forest land other than timberland and productive reserved forest land. It includes available and reserved forest land that is incapable of producing annually 20 cubic feet per acre of industrial wood under natural conditions because of adverse site conditions such as sterile soils, dry climate, poor drainage, high elevation, steepness, or rockiness.

**Other products.** A miscellaneous category of roundwood products, e.g., cooperage, excelsior, shingles, and mill residue byproducts (charcoal, bedding, mulch, etc.).

**Other removals.** The growing-stock volume of trees removed from the inventory by cultural operations such as timber stand improvement, land clearing, and other changes in land use, resulting in the removal of the trees from timberland.

**Other sources.** (See: Nongrowing-stock sources.)

**Ownership.** The property owned by one ownership unit, including all parcels of land in the United States.

*National forest land.* Federal land that has been legally designated as national forests or purchase units, and other land under the administration of the Forest Service, including experimental areas and Bankhead-Jones Title III land.

*Forest industry land.* Land owned by companies or individuals operating primary wood-using plants.

*Nonindustrial private forest (NIPF) land.* Privately owned land excluding forest industry land.

Corporate. Owned by corporations, including incorporated farm ownerships.

Individual. All lands owned by individuals, including farm operators.

*Other public.* An ownership class that includes all public lands except national forests.

Miscellaneous Federal land. Federal land other than national forests.

State, county, and municipal land. Land owned by States, counties, and local public agencies or municipalities, or land leased to these governmental units for 50 years or more.

**Plant residues.** Wood material generated in the production of timber products at primary manufacturing plants.

*Coarse residues.* Material, such as slabs, edgings, trim, veneer cores and ends, which is suitable for chipping.

*Fine residues.* Material, such as sawdust, shavings, and veneer residue, which is not suitable for chipping.

*Plant byproducts.* Residues (coarse or fine) used in the further manufacture of industrial products for consumer use, or as fuel.

*Unused plant residues.* Residues (coarse or fine) that are not used for any product, including fuel.

**Poletimber-size trees.** Softwoods 5.0 to 8.9 inches d.b.h. and hardwoods 5.0 to 10.9 inches d.b.h.

**Posts, poles, and pilings.** Roundwood products milled (cut or peeled) into standard sizes (lengths and circumferences) to be put in the ground to provide vertical and lateral support in buildings, foundations, utility lines, and fences. May also include nonindustrial (unmilled) products.

**Primary wood-using plants.** Industries that convert roundwood products (saw logs, veneer logs, pulpwood, etc.) into primary wood products, such as lumber, veneer or sheathing, wood pulp.

**Production.** The total volume of known roundwood harvested from land within a State, regardless of where it is consumed. Production is the sum of timber harvested and used within a State, and all roundwood exported to other States.

**Pulpwood.** A roundwood product that will be reduced to individual wood fibers by chemical or mechanical means. The fibers are used to make a broad generic group of pulp products that includes paper products, as well as fiberboard, insulating board, and paperboard.

**Receipts.** The quantity or volume of industrial roundwood received at a mill or by a group of mills in a State, regardless of the geographic source. Volume of roundwood receipts is equal to the volume of roundwood retained in a State plus roundwood imported from other States.

**Retained.** Roundwood volume harvested from and processed by mills within the same State.

**Rotten trees.** Live trees of commercial species not containing at least one 12-foot saw log, or two noncontiguous saw logs, each 8 feet or longer, now or prospectively, primarily because of rot or missing sections, and with less than one-third of the gross board-foot tree volume in sound material.

**Rough trees.** Live trees of commercial species not containing at least one 12-foot saw log, or two noncontiguous saw logs, each 8 feet or longer, now or prospectively, primarily because of roughness, poor form, splits, and cracks, and with less than one-third of the gross board-foot tree volume in sound material; and live trees of noncommercial species.

**Roundwood (roundwood logs).** Logs, bolts, or other round sections cut from trees for industrial manufacture or consumer uses.

**Roundwood chipped.** Any timber cut primarily for industrial manufacture, delivered to nonpulpmills, chipped, and then sold to pulpmills for use as fiber. Includes tops, jump sections, whole trees, and pulpwood sticks.

**Roundwood product drain.** That portion of total drain used for a product.

**Roundwood products.** Any primary product, such as lumber, veneer, composite panels, poles, pilings, pulp, or fuelwood that is produced from roundwood.

**Salvable dead trees.** Standing or downed dead trees that were formerly growing stock and considered merchantable. Trees must be at least 5.0 inches d.b.h. to qualify.

**Saplings.** Live trees 1.0 to 5.0 inches d.b.h.

**Saw log.** A roundwood product, usually 8 feet in length or longer, processed into a variety of sawn products such as lumber, cants, pallets, railroad ties, and timbers.

**Saw-log portion.** The part of the bole of sawtimber trees between a 1-foot stump and the saw-log top.

**Saw-log top.** The point on the bole of sawtimber trees above which a conventional saw log cannot be produced. The minimum saw-log top is 7.0 inches d.o.b. for softwoods and 9.0 inches d.o.b. for hardwoods for FIA standards.

**Sawtimber-size trees.** Softwoods 9.0 inches d.b.h. and larger and hardwoods 11.0 inches d.b.h. and larger.

**Sawtimber volume.** Growing-stock volume in the saw-log portion of sawtimber-sized trees in board feet (International ¼-inch rule).

**Seedlings.** Trees < 1.0 inch d.b.h. and > 1 foot tall for hardwoods, > 6 inches tall for softwoods, and > 0.5 inch in diameter at ground level for longleaf pine.

**Select red oaks.** A group of several red oak species composed of cherrybark, Shumard, and northern red oaks. Other red oak species are included in the "other red oaks" group.

**Select white oaks.** A group of several white oak species composed of white, swamp chestnut, swamp white, chinkapin, Durand, and bur oaks. Other white oak species are included in the "other white oaks" group.

**Softwoods.** Coniferous trees, usually evergreen, having leaves that are needles or scale like.

**Standard cord.** A unit of measure applied to roundwood, usually bolts or split wood. It is a stack of wood 4 feet high, 4 feet wide, and 8 feet long encompassing 128 cubic feet of wood, bark, and air space. This usually translates to approximately 75.0 to 81.0 cubic feet of solid wood for pulpwood, because pulpwood is more uniform.

**Standard unit.** A unit measure applied to roundwood timber products. Board feet (International ¼-inch rule) is the standard unit used for saw logs and veneer; cords are used for pulpwood, composite panel, and fuelwood; hundred pieces for poles; thousand pieces for posts; and thousand cubic feet for all other miscellaneous forest products.

**Timberland.** Forest land capable of producing 20 cubic feet of industrial wood per acre per year and not withdrawn from timber utilization.

**Timber product output.** The total volume of roundwood products from all sources plus the volume of byproducts recovered from mill residues (equals roundwood product drain).

**Timber products.** Roundwood products and byproducts.

**Timber removals.** The total volume of trees removed from the timberland inventory by harvesting, cultural operations such as stand improvement, land clearing, or changes in land use. (Note: Includes roundwood products, logging residues, and other removals.)

**Tree.** Woody plants having one erect perennial stem or trunk at least 3 inches d.b.h., a more or less definitely formed crown of foliage, and a height of at least 13 feet (at maturity).

**Upper-stem portion.** The part of the main stem of sawtimber trees above the saw-log top and the minimum top diameter of 4.0 inches outside bark, or to the point where the main stem breaks into limbs.

**Utilization studies.** Studies conducted on active logging operations to develop factors for merchantable portions of trees left in the woods (logging residues), logging damage, and utilization of the unmerchantable portion of growing-stock trees and nongrowing-stock trees.

**Veneer log.** A roundwood product either rotary cut, sliced, stamped, or sawn into a variety of veneer products such as plywood, finished panels, veneer sheets, or sheathing.

**Weight.** A unit of measure for mill residues, expressed as oven-dry tons (2,000 oven-dry pounds).

## Conversion Factors[a]

| | | |
|---|---|---|
| Saw logs | | |
| | Softwood | 0.18282 cubic foot = 1 board foot |
| | | 5.47 board feet = 1 cubic foot |
| | Hardwood | 0.16393 cubic foot = 1 board foot |
| | | 6.10 board feet = 1 cubic foot |
| Veneer logs | | |
| | Softwood | 0.16129 cubic foot = 1 board foot |
| | | 6.20 board feet = 1 cubic foot |
| | Hardwood | 0.16000 cubic foot = 1 board foot |
| | | 6.25 board feet = 1 cubic foot |
| Pulpwood[b] | | |
| | Softwood | 73.3 cubic feet per cord |
| | Hardwood | 76.1 cubic feet per cord |

[a] Conversion factors vary with stem size (d.b.h.) and species. The factors shown are for trees of average diameters removed in Kentucky during the most recent survey period.

[b] Cubic feet of solid wood per cord.

## Species List[a]

| Common name | Scientific name[b] | Common name | Scientific name[b] |
|---|---|---|---|
| **Softwoods** | | **Hardwoods (continued)** | |
| Eastern redcedar | *Juniperus virginiana* L. | Black walnut | *Juglans nigra* L. |
| Shortleaf pine | *Pinus echinata* Mill. | Sweetgum | *Liquidambar styraciflua* L. |
| Table Mt. pine | *P. pungens* Lamb. | Yellow-poplar | *Liriodendron tulipifera* L. |
| Eastern white pine | *P. strobus* L. | Osage-orange | *Maclura pomifera* (Raf.) Schneid. |
| Loblolly pine | *P. taeda* L. | Cucumbertree | *Magnolia acuminata* L. |
| Virginia pine | *P. virginiana* Mill. | Southern magnolia | *M. grandiflora* L. |
| Baldcypress | *Taxodium distichum* (L.) Rich. | Bigleaf magnolia | *M. macrophylla* Michx. |
| Eastern hemlock | *Tsuga canadensis* (L.) Carr. | Apple | *Malus* spp. Mill. |
| | | Chinaberry | *Melia azedarach* L. |
| **Hardwoods** | | White mulberry | *Morus alba* L. |
| Boxelder | *Acer negundo* L. | Red mulberry | *M. rubra* L. |
| Red maple | *A. rubrum* L. | Water tupelo | *Nyssa aquatica* L. |
| Silver maple | *A. saccharinum* L. | Blackgum | *N. sylvatica* Marsh. |
| Sugar maple | *A. saccharum* Marsh. | Swamp tupelo | *N. sylvatica* var. *biflora* (Walt.) Sarg. |
| Buckeye | *Aesculus* spp. L. | Eastern hophornbeam | *Ostrya virginiana* (Mill.) K. Koch |
| Ohio buckeye | *A. glabra* Willd. | Sourwood | *Oxydendrum arboreum* (L.) DC. |
| Ailanthus | *Ailanthus altissima* (Mill.) Swingle | American sycamore | *Platanus occidentalis* L. |
| Serviceberry | *Amelanchier* spp. Medic. | Cottonwood | *Populus* spp. L. |
| Yellow birch | *Betula alleghaniensis* Britton | Black cherry | *Prunus serotina* Ehrh. |
| River birch | *Betula nigra* L. | White oak | *Quercus alba* L. |
| American hornbeam | *Carpinus caroliniana* Walt. | Scarlet oak | *Q. coccinea* Muenchh. |
| Hickory | *Carya* spp. Nutt. | Durand oak | *Q. durandii* Buckl. |
| Water hickory | *C. aquatica* (Michx. f.) Nutt. | Southern red oak | *Q. falcata* Michx. |
| Bitternut hickory | *C. cordiformis* (Wangenh.) K. Koch | Cherrybark oak | *Q. falcata* var. *pagodifolia* Ell. |
| Pignut hickory | *C. glabra* (Mill.) Sweet | Overcup oak | *Q. lyrata* Walt. |
| Pecan | *C. illinoensis* (Wangenh.) K. Koch | Swamp chestnut oak | *Q. michauxii* Nutt. |
| Shellbark hickory | *C. laciniosa* (Michx. f.) Loud. | Chinkapin oak | *Q. muehlenbergii* Engelm. |
| Nutmeg hickory | *C. myristiciformis* (Mich. f.) Nutt. | Water oak | *Q. nigra* L. |
| Shagbark hickory | *C. ovata* (Mill.) K. Koch | Nuttall oak | *Q. nuttallii* Palmer |
| Black hickory | *C. texana* Buckl. | Pin oak | *Q. palustris* Muenchh. |
| Mockernut hickory | *C. tomentosa* (Poir.) Nutt. | Willow oak | *Q. phellos* L. |
| Allegheny chinkapin | *Castanea pumila* Mill. | Chestnut oak | *Q. prinus* L. |
| Chinkapin | *Castanopsis* (D. Don) Spach | Northern red oak | *Q. rubra* L. |
| Catalpa | *Catalpa* spp. Scop. | Shumard oak | *Q. shumardii* Buckl. |
| Sugarberry | *Celtis laevigata* Willd. | Post oak | *Q. stellata* Wangenh. |
| Hackberry | *C. occidentalis* L. | Black oak | *Q. velutina* Lam. |
| Eastern redbud | *Cercis canadensis* L. | Black locust | *Robinia pseudoacacia* L. |
| Flowering dogwood | *Cornus florida* L. | Willow | *Salix* spp. L. |
| Hawthorn | *Crataegus* spp. L. | Sassafras | *Sassafras albidum* (Nutt.) Nees |
| Common persimmon | *Diospyros virginiana* L. | American basswood | *Tilia americana* L. |
| American beech | *Fagus grandifolia* Ehrh. | White basswood | *T. heterophylla* Vent. |
| White ash | *Fraxinus americana* L. | Winged elm | *Ulmus alata* Michx. |
| Pumpkin ash | *F. profunda* (Bush) Bush | American elm | *U. americana* L. |
| Blue ash | *F. quadrangulata* Michx. | Cedar elm | *U. crassifolia* Nutt. |
| Waterlocust | *Gleditsia aquatica* Marsh. | Slippery elm | *U. rubra* Muhl. |
| Honeylocust | *G. triacanthos* L. | September elm | *U. serotina* Sarg.S |
| Kentucky coffeetree | *Gymnocladus dioicus* (L.) K. Koch | Rock elm | *U. thomasii* Sarg. |
| American holly | *Ilex opaca* Ait. | | |

[a] Common and scientific names of tree species ≥1.0 inch d.b.h. occurring in the FIA sample.
[b] Little (1979).

# Appendix

## Index of Tables

**Table A.1—Output of industrial products by product and species group, Kentucky, 2005 and 2007**

| Product and species group | Year 2005 | Year 2007 | Change | Change |
|---|---|---|---|---|
| | - - - - - thousand cubic feet - - - - - | | | *percent* |
| **Saw logs** | | | | |
| Softwood | 4,429 | 4,164 | -265 | -6.0 |
| Hardwood | 138,870 | 140,254 | 1,384 | 1.0 |
| Total | 143,299 | 144,418 | 1,119 | 0.8 |
| **Veneer logs** | | | | |
| Softwood | 268 | 7 | -261 | -97.4 |
| Hardwood | 7,280 | 6,538 | -742 | -10.2 |
| Total | 7,548 | 6,545 | -1,003 | -13.3 |
| **Pulpwood** | | | | |
| Softwood | 4,162 | 4,187 | 25 | 0.6 |
| Hardwood | 20,389 | 20,420 | 31 | 0.2 |
| Total | 24,551 | 24,607 | 56 | 0.2 |
| **Composite panels** | | | | |
| Softwood | 2,038 | 1,929 | -109 | -5.3 |
| Hardwood | 12,061 | 6,946 | -5,115 | -42.4 |
| Total | 14,099 | 8,875 | -5,224 | -37.1 |
| **Other industrial** | | | | |
| Softwood | 1,639 | 1,251 | -388 | -23.7 |
| Hardwood | 44 | 0 | -44 | -100.0 |
| Total | 1,683 | 1,251 | -432 | -25.7 |
| **All industrial** | | | | |
| Softwood | 12,536 | 11,538 | -998 | -8.0 |
| Hardwood | 178,644 | 174,158 | -4,486 | -2.5 |
| Total | 191,180 | 185,696 | -5,484 | -2.9 |

[a] Includes roundwood delivered to nonpulpmills, then chipped and sold to pulpmills (373,000 cubic feet in 2005 and 140,000 cubic feet in 2007).

**Table A.2—Roundwood receipts by product and species group, Kentucky, 2005 and 2007**

| Product and species group | Year | | Change | Change |
|---|---|---|---|---|
| | 2005 | 2007 | | |
| | - - - - - thousand cubic feet - - - - - | | | percent |
| Saw logs | | | | |
| Softwood | 4,172 | 4,225 | 53 | 1.3 |
| Hardwood | 140,738 | 135,976 | -4,762 | -3.4 |
| Total | 144,910 | 140,201 | -4,709 | -3.2 |
| Veneer logs | | | | |
| Softwood | 0 | 9 | 9 | 100.0 |
| Hardwood | 1,950 | 1,500 | -450 | -23.1 |
| Total | 1,950 | 1,509 | -441 | -22.6 |
| Pulpwood[a] | | | | |
| Softwood | 2,317 | 2,454 | 137 | 5.9 |
| Hardwood | 53,311 | 48,893 | -4,418 | -8.3 |
| Total | 55,628 | 51,347 | -4,281 | -7.7 |
| Other industrial | | | | |
| Softwood | 1,772 | 1,257 | -515 | -29.1 |
| Hardwood | 10,120 | 5,506 | -4,614 | -45.6 |
| Total | 11,892 | 6,763 | -5,129 | -43.1 |
| Total output | | | | |
| Softwood | 8,261 | 7,945 | -316 | -3.8 |
| Hardwood | 206,119 | 191,875 | -14,244 | -6.9 |
| Total | 214,380 | 199,820 | -14,560 | -6.8 |

[a] Includes roundwood delivered to nonpulpmills, then chipped and sold to pulpmills (373,000 cubic feet in 2005 and 143,000 cubic feet in 2007).

**Table A.3—Number of primary wood-using plants by type of mill, Kentucky, 1969 to 2007**

| Type of mill | Year | | | | | | | | | |
|---|---|---|---|---|---|---|---|---|---|---|
| | 1969 | 1974 | 1986 | 1995 | 1997 | 1999 | 2003 | 2005 | 2005 | 2007 |
| | number | | | | | | | | | |
| Sawmills | 538 | 388 | 408 | 376 | 365 | 330 | 317 | 282 | 277 | 241 |
| Veneer or plywood mills | 4 | 4 | 3 | 3 | 4 | 3 | 3 | 3 | 3 | 3 |
| Pulpmills | 2 | 2 | 2 | 2 | 2 | 2 | 2 | 2 | 2 | 2 |
| Composite panel mills | 0 | 0 | 0 | 1 | 1 | 1 | 1 | 1 | 1 | 1 |
| Other mills | 45 | 26 | 22 | 19 | 19 | 12 | 14 | 9 | 9 | 6 |
| All plants | 589 | 420 | 435 | 401 | 391 | 348 | 337 | 297 | 292 | 253 |

**Table A.4—Roundwood receipts by sawmill size, Kentucky, 2005 and 2007**

| Sawmill size class[a] | 2005 | | | 2007 | | |
|---|---|---|---|---|---|---|
| | Mills | Volume | | Mills | Volume | |
| mmbf | number | mbf | percent | number | mbf | percent |
| <1.0 | 114 | 35,550 | 4 | 94 | 26,709 | 3 |
| 1.0–4.99 | 110 | 283,094 | 32 | 101 | 286,706 | 34 |
| 5.0–9.99 | 35 | 237,688 | 27 | 26 | 177,080 | 21 |
| >10 | 18 | 325,083 | 37 | 20 | 362,138 | 42 |
| Total | 277 | 881,415 | 100 | 241 | 852,633 | 100 |

[a] Based on volume received as opposed to actual capacity.

**Table A.5—Roundwood receipts by species and type of mill, Kentucky, 2007**

| | | | Type of mill | | | |
|---|---|---|---|---|---|---|
| | | | Veneer mills | | | |
| Species | All mills | Sawmills | Pine plywood | Other veneer | Pulpmills[a] | Other mills |
| | | | thousand cubic feet | | | |
| Softwood | | | | | | |
| Yellow pine | 2,241 | 2,010 | 0 | 4 | NA | 227 |
| White pine | 531 | 402 | 0 | 0 | NA | 129 |
| Cedar | 2,258 | 1,404 | 0 | 5 | NA | 849 |
| Cypress | 96 | 96 | 0 | 0 | NA | 0 |
| Other softwood | 365 | 313 | 0 | 0 | NA | 52 |
| Unclassified | 2,454 | 0 | 0 | 0 | 2,454 | 0 |
| Total softwoods | 7,945 | 4,225 | 0 | 9 | 2,454 | 1,257 |
| Hardwood | | | | | | |
| Blackgum-tupelo | 565 | 565 | 0 | 0 | NA | 0 |
| Soft maple | 5,137 | 4,417 | 0 | 4 | NA | 716 |
| Sweetgum | 696 | 696 | 0 | 0 | NA | 0 |
| Yellow-poplar | 31,711 | 27,508 | 0 | 18 | NA | 4,185 |
| Other soft hardwood | 5,701 | 5,261 | 0 | 0 | NA | 440 |
| Hickory | 9,306 | 9,269 | 0 | 37 | NA | 0 |
| Red oak | 33,066 | 32,322 | 0 | 744 | NA | 0 |
| White oak | 28,899 | 28,752 | 0 | 147 | NA | 0 |
| Other hard hardwood | 27,901 | 27,186 | 0 | 550 | NA | 165 |
| Unclassified | 48,893 | 0 | 0 | 0 | 48,893 | 0 |
| Total hardwoods | 191,875 | 135,976 | 0 | 1,500 | 48,893 | 5,506 |
| All species | 199,820 | 140,201 | 0 | 1,509 | 51,347 | 6,763 |

NA = not applicable.

[a] Collected only by softwood and hardwood and includes roundwood chipped.

**Table A.6—Industrial roundwood movement by year and species group, Kentucky, 2005 and 2007**

| Year | Production | Exported to other States | Retained | Imported from other States | Receipts |
|---|---|---|---|---|---|
| | | | *thousand cubic feet* | | |
| | | | **Softwood** | | |
| 2005 | 12,536 | 5,755 | 6,781 | 1,480 | 8,261 |
| 2007 | 11,538 | 5,392 | 6,146 | 1,799 | 7,945 |
| | | | **Hardwood** | | |
| 2005 | 178,644 | 21,015 | 157,629 | 48,490 | 206,119 |
| 2007 | 174,158 | 23,135 | 151,023 | 40,852 | 191,875 |
| | | | **All species** | | |
| 2005 | 191,180 | 26,770 | 164,410 | 49,970 | 214,380 |
| 2007 | 185,696 | 28,527 | 157,169 | 42,651 | 199,820 |

**Table A.7—Industrial roundwood movement by product and species group, Kentucky, 2007**

| Product and species group | Production | Exported to other States | Retained | Imported from other States | Receipts |
|---|---|---|---|---|---|
| | | | *thousand cubic feet* | | |
| Saw logs | | | | | |
| Softwood | 4,164 | 464 | 3,700 | 525 | 4,225 |
| Hardwood | 140,254 | 12,237 | 128,017 | 7,959 | 135,976 |
| Total | 144,418 | 12,701 | 131,717 | 8,484 | 140,201 |
| Veneer logs | | | | | |
| Softwood | 7 | 3 | 4 | 5 | 9 |
| Hardwood | 6,538 | 6,064 | 474 | 1,026 | 1,500 |
| Total | 6,545 | 6,067 | 478 | 1,031 | 1,509 |
| Pulpwood[a] | | | | | |
| Softwood | 4,187 | 2,905 | 1,282 | 1,172 | 2,454 |
| Hardwood | 20,420 | 3,394 | 17,026 | 31,867 | 48,893 |
| Total | 24,607 | 6,299 | 18,308 | 33,039 | 51,347 |
| Other industrial | | | | | |
| Softwood | 3,180 | 2,020 | 1,160 | 97 | 1,257 |
| Hardwood | 6,946 | 1,440 | 5,506 | 0 | 5,506 |
| Total | 10,126 | 3,460 | 6,666 | 97 | 6,763 |
| All products | | | | | |
| Softwood | 11,538 | 5,392 | 6,146 | 1,799 | 7,945 |
| Hardwood | 174,158 | 23,135 | 151,023 | 40,852 | 191,875 |
| Total | 185,696 | 28,527 | 157,169 | 42,651 | 199,820 |

[a] Includes roundwood delivered to nonpulpmills, then chipped and sold to pulpmills.

**Table A.8—Saw-log volume by destination, source, and species group, Kentucky, 2007**

| Destination and source | All species | Species group | |
|---|---|---|---|
| | | Softwood | Hardwood |
| | *thousand cubic feet* | | |
| Kentucky (retained) | 131,717 | 3,700 | 128,017 |
| Exports to | | | |
| Alabama | 75 | 75 | 0 |
| Indiana | 3,011 | 52 | 2,959 |
| Missouri | 590 | 0 | 590 |
| Ohio | 5,239 | 58 | 5,181 |
| Tennessee | 2,682 | 60 | 2,622 |
| Virginia | 1,104 | 219 | 885 |
| Total | 12,701 | 464 | 12,237 |
| Imports from | | | |
| Illinois | 155 | 50 | 105 |
| Indiana | 304 | 24 | 280 |
| Missouri | 92 | 50 | 42 |
| North Carolina | 3 | 3 | 0 |
| Ohio | 32 | 0 | 32 |
| South Carolina | 8 | 8 | 0 |
| Tennessee | 6,250 | 390 | 5,860 |
| Virginia | 740 | 0 | 740 |
| West Virginia | 900 | 0 | 900 |
| Total | 8,484 | 525 | 7,959 |

**Table A.9—Veneer volume by destination, source, and species group, Kentucky, 2007**

| Destination and source | All species | Species group | |
|---|---|---|---|
| | | Softwood | Hardwood |
| | *thousand cubic feet* | | |
| Kentucky (retained) | 478 | 4 | 474 |
| Exports to | | | |
| Georgia | 3,364 | 0 | 3,364 |
| Indiana | 575 | 3 | 572 |
| Michigan | 145 | 0 | 145 |
| North Carolina | 1,784 | 0 | 1,784 |
| Wisconsin | 199 | 0 | 199 |
| Total | 6,067 | 3 | 6,064 |
| Imports from | | | |
| Illinois | 11 | 0 | 11 |
| Indiana | 184 | 0 | 184 |
| Maine | 12 | 0 | 12 |
| Michigan | 149 | 0 | 149 |
| New York | 48 | 0 | 48 |
| Ohio | 154 | 0 | 154 |
| Pennsylvania | 112 | 0 | 112 |
| Texas | 5 | 5 | 0 |
| Washington | 38 | 0 | 38 |
| West Virginia | 318 | 0 | 318 |
| Total | 1,031 | 5 | 1,026 |

**Table A.10—Pulpwood volume by destination, source, and species group, Kentucky, 2007**[a]

| Destination and source | All species | Species group | |
|---|---|---|---|
| | | Softwood | Hardwood |
| | *thousand cubic feet* | | |
| Kentucky (retained) | 18,308 | 1,282 | 17,026 |
| Exports to | | | |
| Ohio | 2,369 | 1,873 | 496 |
| Tennessee | 3,888 | 1,032 | 2,856 |
| Virginia | 42 | 0 | 42 |
| Total | 6,299 | 2,905 | 3,394 |
| Imports from | | | |
| Alabama | 1,563 | 0 | 1,563 |
| Arkansas | 505 | 0 | 505 |
| Illinois | 1,157 | 185 | 972 |
| Indiana | 1,500 | 0 | 1,500 |
| Mississippi | 9,879 | 0 | 9,879 |
| Missouri | 2,827 | 0 | 2,827 |
| North Carolina | 46 | 0 | 46 |
| Tennessee | 15,521 | 987 | 14,534 |
| Virginia | 41 | 0 | 41 |
| Total | 33,039 | 1,172 | 31,867 |

[a] Includes roundwood delivered to nonpulpmills, then chipped and sold to pulpmills.

**Table A.11—Other industrial volume by destination, source, and species group, Kentucky, 2007**[a]

| Destination and source | All species | Species group | |
|---|---|---|---|
| | | Softwood | Hardwood |
| | *thousand cubic feet* | | |
| Kentucky (retained) | 6,666 | 1,160 | 5,506 |
| Exports to | | | |
| Alabama | 42 | 42 | 0 |
| Indiana | 49 | 49 | 0 |
| Tennessee | 2,566 | 1,828 | 738 |
| West Virginia | 803 | 101 | 702 |
| Total | 3,460 | 2,020 | 1,440 |
| Imports from | | | |
| Indiana | 11 | 11 | 0 |
| Tennesse | 43 | 43 | 0 |
| Virginia | 43 | 43 | 0 |
| Total | 97 | 97 | 0 |

[a] Includes poles, posts, mulch, firewood, log homes, charcoal, composite panel, and all other industrial mills.

**Table A.12—Primary mill residue volume by roundwood type, species group, and residue type, Kentucky, 2007**

| Roundwood type and species group | All types | Residue type | | | |
|---|---|---|---|---|---|
| | | Bark | Coarse | Sawdust | Shavings |
| | | *thousand cubic feet* | | | |
| Saw logs | | | | | |
| Softwood | 2,181 | 284 | 1,136 | 753 | 8 |
| Hardwood | 79,279 | 14,172 | 37,119 | 27,517 | 471 |
| Total | 81,460 | 14,456 | 38,255 | 28,270 | 479 |
| Veneer logs | | | | | |
| Softwood | 6 | 1 | 4 | 1 | 0 |
| Hardwood | 615 | 179 | 288 | 148 | 0 |
| Total | 621 | 180 | 292 | 149 | 0 |
| Pulpwood | | | | | |
| Softwood | 265 | 265 | 0 | 0 | 0 |
| Hardwood | 6,115 | 6,115 | 0 | 0 | 0 |
| Total | 6,380 | 6,380 | 0 | 0 | 0 |
| Other industrial[a] | | | | | |
| Softwood | 576 | 133 | 316 | 127 | 0 |
| Hardwood | 1,241 | 1,239 | 1 | 1 | 0 |
| Total | 1,817 | 1,372 | 317 | 128 | 0 |
| Total | | | | | |
| Softwood | 3028 | 683 | 1,456 | 881 | 8 |
| Hardwood | 87,250 | 21,705 | 37,408 | 27,666 | 471 |
| Total | 90,278 | 22,388 | 38,864 | 28,547 | 479 |

[a] Includes poles, pilings, posts, and all other industrial products.

**Table A.13—Disposal of residue at primary wood-using plants by product, species group, and type of residue, Kentucky, 2005 and 2007**

| Product and species group | All types 2005 | All types 2007 | Bark 2005 | Bark 2007 | Coarse 2005 | Coarse 2007 | Sawdust 2005 | Sawdust 2007 | Shavings 2005 | Shavings 2007 |
|---|---|---|---|---|---|---|---|---|---|---|
| | *thousand cubic feet* | | | | | | | | | |
| **Fiber products** | | | | | | | | | | |
| Softwood | 173 | 190 | 0 | 0 | 173 | 190 | 0 | 0 | 0 | 0 |
| Hardwood | 21,160 | 19,801 | 0 | 0 | 21,108 | 19,801 | 52 | 0 | 0 | 0 |
| Total | 21,333 | 19,991 | 0 | 0 | 21,281 | 19,991 | 52 | 0 | 0 | 0 |
| **Particleboard** | | | | | | | | | | |
| Softwood | 88 | 57 | 0 | 0 | 42 | 31 | 46 | 26 | 0 | 0 |
| Hardwood | 2,890 | 2,483 | 307 | 47 | 2,492 | 2,413 | 79 | 0 | 12 | 23 |
| Total | 2,978 | 2,540 | 307 | 47 | 2,534 | 2,444 | 125 | 26 | 12 | 23 |
| **Charcoal/ chemical wood** | | | | | | | | | | |
| Softwood | 156 | 116 | 0 | 6 | 46 | 30 | 106 | 80 | 4 | 0 |
| Hardwood | 12,094 | 16,214 | 1,166 | 1,957 | 2,539 | 6,979 | 8,290 | 7,277 | 99 | 1 |
| Total | 12,250 | 16,330 | 1,166 | 1,963 | 2,585 | 7,009 | 8,396 | 7,357 | 103 | 1 |
| **Sawn products** | | | | | | | | | | |
| Softwood | 0 | 4 | 0 | 0 | 0 | 4 | 0 | 0 | 0 | 0 |
| Hardwood | 1,088 | 43 | 0 | 0 | 1,088 | 43 | 0 | 0 | 0 | 0 |
| Total | 1,088 | 47 | 0 | 0 | 1,088 | 47 | 0 | 0 | 0 | 0 |
| **Industrial fuel** | | | | | | | | | | |
| Softwood | 528 | 858 | 278 | 344 | 156 | 316 | 94 | 198 | 0 | 0 |
| Hardwood | 28,963 | 27,397 | 10,480 | 8,444 | 5,885 | 3,897 | 12,574 | 14,849 | 24 | 207 |
| Total | 29,491 | 28,255 | 10,758 | 8,788 | 6,041 | 4,213 | 12,668 | 15,047 | 24 | 207 |
| **Miscellaneous** | | | | | | | | | | |
| Softwood | 1,843 | 1,686 | 371 | 326 | 981 | 789 | 480 | 563 | 11 | 8 |
| Hardwood | 22,307 | 19,633 | 11,293 | 10,929 | 4,414 | 3,648 | 6,308 | 4,816 | 292 | 240 |
| Total | 24,150 | 21,319 | 11,664 | 11,255 | 5,395 | 4,437 | 6,788 | 5,379 | 303 | 248 |
| **Not used** | | | | | | | | | | |
| Softwood | 375 | 117 | 52 | 7 | 148 | 96 | 174 | 14 | 1 | 0 |
| Hardwood | 3,297 | 1,679 | 495 | 328 | 1,365 | 627 | 1,436 | 724 | 1 | 0 |
| Total | 3,672 | 1,796 | 547 | 335 | 1,513 | 723 | 1,610 | 738 | 2 | 0 |
| **All products** | | | | | | | | | | |
| Softwood | 3,163 | 3,028 | 701 | 683 | 1,546 | 1,456 | 900 | 881 | 16 | 8 |
| Hardwood | 91,799 | 87,250 | 23,741 | 21,705 | 38,891 | 37,408 | 28,739 | 27,666 | 428 | 471 |
| Total | 94,962 | 90,278 | 24,442 | 22,388 | 40,437 | 38,864 | 29,639 | 28,547 | 444 | 479 |

**Table A.14—Roundwood timber product output by county, product, and species group, Kentucky, 2007**

| County | All products Soft-wood | All products Hard-wood | Saw logs Soft-wood | Saw logs Hard-wood | Veneer logs Soft-wood | Veneer logs Hard-wood | Pulpwood[a] Soft-wood | Pulpwood[a] Hard-wood | Composite panels Soft-wood | Composite panels Hard-wood | Other industrial Soft-wood | Other industrial Hard-wood |
|---|---|---|---|---|---|---|---|---|---|---|---|---|
| | | | | | *thousand cubic feet* | | | | | | | |
| Adair | 31 | 3,532 | 31 | 3,527 | 0 | 0 | 0 | 5 | 0 | 0 | 0 | 0 |
| Allen | 0 | 3,698 | 0 | 3,688 | 0 | 0 | 0 | 10 | 0 | 0 | 0 | 0 |
| Anderson | 48 | 30 | 48 | 30 | 0 | 0 | 0 | 0 | 0 | 0 | 0 | 0 |
| Ballard | 0 | 1,535 | 0 | 787 | 0 | 0 | 0 | 748 | 0 | 0 | 0 | 0 |
| Barren | 27 | 1,843 | 27 | 1,843 | 0 | 0 | 0 | 0 | 0 | 0 | 0 | 0 |
| Bath | 28 | 295 | 24 | 295 | 0 | 0 | 0 | 0 | 0 | 0 | 4 | 0 |
| Bell | 0 | 3,902 | 0 | 3,902 | 0 | 0 | 0 | 0 | 0 | 0 | 0 | 0 |
| Boone | 0 | 165 | 0 | 165 | 0 | 0 | 0 | 0 | 0 | 0 | 0 | 0 |
| Bourbon | 0 | 148 | 0 | 0 | 0 | 148 | 0 | 0 | 0 | 0 | 0 | 0 |
| Boyd | 0 | 724 | 0 | 724 | 0 | 0 | 0 | 0 | 0 | 0 | 0 | 0 |
| Boyle | 0 | 155 | 0 | 155 | 0 | 0 | 0 | 0 | 0 | 0 | 0 | 0 |
| Bracken | 0 | 1,041 | 0 | 1,041 | 0 | 0 | 0 | 0 | 0 | 0 | 0 | 0 |
| Breathitt | 0 | 2,501 | 0 | 1,111 | 0 | 437 | 0 | 0 | 0 | 953 | 0 | 0 |
| Breckinridge | 87 | 4,029 | 35 | 2,409 | 1 | 228 | 0 | 1,392 | 0 | 0 | 51 | 0 |
| Bullitt | 126 | 157 | 54 | 157 | 0 | 0 | 0 | 0 | 0 | 0 | 72 | 0 |
| Butler | 26 | 1,767 | 26 | 1,744 | 0 | 18 | 0 | 5 | 0 | 0 | 0 | 0 |
| Caldwell | 261 | 1,991 | 261 | 1,402 | 0 | 0 | 0 | 589 | 0 | 0 | 0 | 0 |
| Calloway | 413 | 755 | 9 | 616 | 0 | 0 | 404 | 139 | 0 | 0 | 0 | 0 |
| Campbell | 56 | 0 | 5 | 0 | 0 | 0 | 0 | 0 | 0 | 0 | 51 | 0 |
| Carlisle | 20 | 1,736 | 20 | 689 | 0 | 0 | 0 | 1,047 | 0 | 0 | 0 | 0 |
| Carroll | 55 | 121 | 4 | 121 | 0 | 0 | 0 | 0 | 0 | 0 | 51 | 0 |
| Carter | 103 | 2,871 | 88 | 2,871 | 0 | 0 | 0 | 0 | 0 | 0 | 15 | 0 |
| Casey | 31 | 4,789 | 31 | 4,778 | 0 | 0 | 0 | 11 | 0 | 0 | 0 | 0 |
| Christian | 605 | 1,806 | 15 | 1,745 | 0 | 0 | 590 | 61 | 0 | 0 | 0 | 0 |
| Clark | 0 | 167 | 0 | 18 | 0 | 149 | 0 | 0 | 0 | 0 | 0 | 0 |
| Clay | 20 | 577 | 10 | 567 | 0 | 0 | 0 | 10 | 0 | 0 | 10 | 0 |
| Clinton | 24 | 1,922 | 24 | 1,922 | 0 | 0 | 0 | 0 | 0 | 0 | 0 | 0 |
| Crittenden | 1,656 | 1,736 | 261 | 812 | 0 | 106 | 481 | 449 | 914 | 369 | 0 | 0 |
| Cumberland | 24 | 3,157 | 24 | 3,157 | 0 | 0 | 0 | 0 | 0 | 0 | 0 | 0 |
| Daviess | 63 | 1,173 | 51 | 1,148 | 0 | 0 | 12 | 25 | 0 | 0 | 0 | 0 |
| Edmonson | 82 | 961 | 82 | 961 | 0 | 0 | 0 | 0 | 0 | 0 | 0 | 0 |
| Elliott | 69 | 968 | 17 | 968 | 0 | 0 | 0 | 0 | 0 | 0 | 52 | 0 |
| Estill | 39 | 1,683 | 39 | 1,683 | 0 | 0 | 0 | 0 | 0 | 0 | 0 | 0 |
| Fayette | 0 | 149 | 0 | 0 | 0 | 149 | 0 | 0 | 0 | 0 | 0 | 0 |
| Fleming | 0 | 1,480 | 0 | 1,480 | 0 | 0 | 0 | 0 | 0 | 0 | 0 | 0 |
| Floyd | 0 | 2,633 | 0 | 2,378 | 0 | 0 | 0 | 0 | 0 | 255 | 0 | 0 |
| Franklin | 79 | 13 | 26 | 13 | 0 | 0 | 0 | 0 | 0 | 0 | 53 | 0 |
| Fulton | 48 | 183 | 48 | 112 | 0 | 0 | 0 | 71 | 0 | 0 | 0 | 0 |
| Gallatin | 0 | 117 | 0 | 117 | 0 | 0 | 0 | 0 | 0 | 0 | 0 | 0 |
| Garrard | 18 | 71 | 18 | 71 | 0 | 0 | 0 | 0 | 0 | 0 | 0 | 0 |
| Grant | 0 | 76 | 0 | 3 | 0 | 73 | 0 | 0 | 0 | 0 | 0 | 0 |
| Graves | 24 | 1,125 | 8 | 746 | 0 | 0 | 16 | 379 | 0 | 0 | 0 | 0 |
| Grayson | 179 | 2,928 | 57 | 2,737 | 0 | 0 | 1 | 191 | 0 | 0 | 121 | 0 |
| Green | 55 | 2,381 | 55 | 2,381 | 0 | 0 | 0 | 0 | 0 | 0 | 0 | 0 |
| Greenup | 144 | 5,936 | 11 | 2,570 | 0 | 0 | 35 | 3,184 | 98 | 182 | 0 | 0 |

*continued*

**Table A.14—Roundwood timber product output by county, product, and species group, Kentucky, 2007 (continued)**

| County | All products Soft-wood | All products Hard-wood | Saw logs Soft-wood | Saw logs Hard-wood | Veneer logs Soft-wood | Veneer logs Hard-wood | Pulpwood[a] Soft-wood | Pulpwood[a] Hard-wood | Composite panels Soft-wood | Composite panels Hard-wood | Other industrial Soft-wood | Other industrial Hard-wood |
|---|---|---|---|---|---|---|---|---|---|---|---|---|
| | | | | | *thousand cubic feet* | | | | | | | |
| Hancock | 0 | 1,138 | 0 | 1,138 | 0 | 0 | 0 | 0 | 0 | 0 | 0 | 0 |
| Hardin | 81 | 1,323 | 78 | 1,273 | 0 | 48 | 3 | 2 | 0 | 0 | 0 | 0 |
| Harlan | 219 | 3,851 | 219 | 2,413 | 0 | 336 | 0 | 0 | 0 | 1,102 | 0 | 0 |
| Hart | 172 | 2,066 | 120 | 2,066 | 0 | 0 | 0 | 0 | 0 | 0 | 52 | 0 |
| Henderson | 0 | 73 | 0 | 73 | 0 | 0 | 0 | 0 | 0 | 0 | 0 | 0 |
| Henry | 164 | 15 | 108 | 15 | 5 | 0 | 0 | 0 | 0 | 0 | 51 | 0 |
| Hickman | 52 | 539 | 39 | 440 | 0 | 0 | 13 | 99 | 0 | 0 | 0 | 0 |
| Hopkins | 56 | 3,199 | 14 | 3,001 | 0 | 0 | 42 | 198 | 0 | 0 | 0 | 0 |
| Jackson | 44 | 845 | 37 | 838 | 0 | 0 | 0 | 7 | 0 | 0 | 7 | 0 |
| Jefferson | 0 | 145 | 0 | 145 | 0 | 0 | 0 | 0 | 0 | 0 | 0 | 0 |
| Johnson | 19 | 1,055 | 19 | 1,055 | 0 | 0 | 0 | 0 | 0 | 0 | 0 | 0 |
| Kenton | 0 | 88 | 0 | 87 | 0 | 1 | 0 | 0 | 0 | 0 | 0 | 0 |
| Knott | 0 | 1,307 | 0 | 1,087 | 0 | 0 | 0 | 0 | 0 | 220 | 0 | 0 |
| Knox | 33 | 8,773 | 20 | 6,034 | 0 | 280 | 5 | 2,263 | 1 | 196 | 7 | 0 |
| Larue | 72 | 601 | 0 | 542 | 0 | 59 | 0 | 0 | 0 | 0 | 72 | 0 |
| Laurel | 278 | 7,776 | 4 | 1,160 | 0 | 1,235 | 246 | 4,189 | 0 | 1,192 | 28 | 0 |
| Lawrence | 16 | 1,615 | 16 | 1,615 | 0 | 0 | 0 | 0 | 0 | 0 | 0 | 0 |
| Lee | 69 | 2,324 | 63 | 2,159 | 0 | 0 | 4 | 0 | 0 | 165 | 2 | 0 |
| Leslie | 29 | 2,913 | 28 | 2,003 | 0 | 0 | 0 | 7 | 1 | 903 | 0 | 0 |
| Letcher | 0 | 1,424 | 0 | 1,389 | 0 | 0 | 0 | 0 | 0 | 35 | 0 | 0 |
| Lewis | 26 | 5,079 | 14 | 5,074 | 0 | 0 | 12 | 5 | 0 | 0 | 0 | 0 |
| Lincoln | 0 | 588 | 0 | 588 | 0 | 0 | 0 | 0 | 0 | 0 | 0 | 0 |
| Livingston | 1,002 | 449 | 10 | 387 | 0 | 0 | 992 | 62 | 0 | 0 | 0 | 0 |
| Logan | 27 | 1,059 | 27 | 1,047 | 0 | 0 | 0 | 12 | 0 | 0 | 0 | 0 |
| Lyon | 452 | 912 | 73 | 738 | 0 | 0 | 379 | 174 | 0 | 0 | 0 | 0 |
| Madison | 0 | 145 | 0 | 145 | 0 | 0 | 0 | 0 | 0 | 0 | 0 | 0 |
| Magoffin | 14 | 774 | 14 | 774 | 0 | 0 | 0 | 0 | 0 | 0 | 0 | 0 |
| Marion | 73 | 1,064 | 22 | 997 | 0 | 67 | 0 | 0 | 0 | 0 | 51 | 0 |
| Marshall | 182 | 815 | 3 | 459 | 0 | 5 | 179 | 351 | 0 | 0 | 0 | 0 |
| Martin | 0 | 873 | 0 | 873 | 0 | 0 | 0 | 0 | 0 | 0 | 0 | 0 |
| Mason | 22 | 1,520 | 22 | 1,520 | 0 | 0 | 0 | 0 | 0 | 0 | 0 | 0 |
| McCracken | 0 | 235 | 0 | 210 | 0 | 0 | 0 | 25 | 0 | 0 | 0 | 0 |
| McCreary | 1,005 | 1,546 | 90 | 471 | 0 | 527 | 0 | 179 | 915 | 369 | 0 | 0 |
| McLean | 0 | 830 | 0 | 742 | 0 | 0 | 0 | 88 | 0 | 0 | 0 | 0 |
| Meade | 35 | 1,187 | 34 | 1,084 | 1 | 103 | 0 | 0 | 0 | 0 | 0 | 0 |
| Menifee | 82 | 927 | 73 | 927 | 0 | 0 | 0 | 0 | 0 | 0 | 9 | 0 |
| Mercer | 33 | 0 | 33 | 0 | 0 | 0 | 0 | 0 | 0 | 0 | 0 | 0 |
| Metcalfe | 30 | 2,433 | 30 | 2,392 | 0 | 0 | 0 | 41 | 0 | 0 | 0 | 0 |
| Monroe | 18 | 3,317 | 18 | 3,297 | 0 | 0 | 0 | 20 | 0 | 0 | 0 | 0 |
| Montgomery | 17 | 107 | 17 | 107 | 0 | 0 | 0 | 0 | 0 | 0 | 0 | 0 |
| Morgan | 97 | 832 | 89 | 832 | 0 | 0 | 0 | 0 | 0 | 0 | 8 | 0 |
| Muhlenberg | 240 | 1,925 | 28 | 1,791 | 0 | 0 | 212 | 134 | 0 | 0 | 0 | 0 |
| Nelson | 165 | 308 | 114 | 308 | 0 | 0 | 0 | 0 | 0 | 0 | 51 | 0 |
| Ohio | 117 | 6,570 | 45 | 2,983 | 0 | 139 | 23 | 3,448 | 0 | 0 | 49 | 0 |
| Oldham | 24 | 79 | 24 | 79 | 0 | 0 | 0 | 0 | 0 | 0 | 0 | 0 |

*continued*

**Table A.14—Roundwood timber product output by county, product, and species group, Kentucky, 2007 (continued)**

| County | All products | | Saw logs | | Veneer logs | | Pulpwood[a] | | Composite panels | | Other industrial | |
|---|---|---|---|---|---|---|---|---|---|---|---|---|
| | Soft-wood | Hard-wood | Soft-wood | Hard-wood | Soft-wood | Hard-wood | Soft-wood | Hard-wood | Soft-wood | Hard-wood | Soft-wood | Hard-wood |
| | *thousand cubic feet* | | | | | | | | | | | |
| Owen | 171 | 198 | 120 | 125 | 0 | 73 | 0 | 0 | 0 | 0 | 51 | 0 |
| Owsley | 0 | 287 | 0 | 287 | 0 | 0 | 0 | 0 | 0 | 0 | 0 | 0 |
| Pendleton | 60 | 16 | 9 | 16 | 0 | 0 | 0 | 0 | 0 | 0 | 51 | 0 |
| Perry | 0 | 1,285 | 0 | 724 | 0 | 0 | 0 | 3 | 0 | 558 | 0 | 0 |
| Pike | 0 | 3,783 | 0 | 2,786 | 0 | 605 | 0 | 0 | 0 | 392 | 0 | 0 |
| Powell | 84 | 884 | 82 | 884 | 0 | 0 | 0 | 0 | 0 | 0 | 2 | 0 |
| Pulaski | 66 | 4,741 | 56 | 4,741 | 0 | 0 | 0 | 0 | 0 | 0 | 10 | 0 |
| Robertson | 10 | 520 | 10 | 520 | 0 | 0 | 0 | 0 | 0 | 0 | 0 | 0 |
| Rockcastle | 20 | 1,362 | 13 | 1,362 | 0 | 0 | 0 | 0 | 0 | 0 | 7 | 0 |
| Rowan | 13 | 1,304 | 1 | 1,224 | 0 | 25 | 0 | 0 | 0 | 55 | 12 | 0 |
| Russell | 28 | 1,529 | 28 | 1,524 | 0 | 0 | 0 | 5 | 0 | 0 | 0 | 0 |
| Scott | 24 | 0 | 24 | 0 | 0 | 0 | 0 | 0 | 0 | 0 | 0 | 0 |
| Shelby | 107 | 172 | 56 | 172 | 0 | 0 | 0 | 0 | 0 | 0 | 51 | 0 |
| Simpson | 0 | 86 | 0 | 86 | 0 | 0 | 0 | 0 | 0 | 0 | 0 | 0 |
| Spencer | 104 | 0 | 53 | 0 | 0 | 0 | 0 | 0 | 0 | 0 | 51 | 0 |
| Taylor | 0 | 3,218 | 0 | 3,218 | 0 | 0 | 0 | 0 | 0 | 0 | 0 | 0 |
| Todd | 0 | 771 | 0 | 771 | 0 | 0 | 0 | 0 | 0 | 0 | 0 | 0 |
| Trigg | 498 | 1,840 | 8 | 1,489 | 0 | 0 | 490 | 351 | 0 | 0 | 0 | 0 |
| Trimble | 195 | 86 | 144 | 86 | 0 | 0 | 0 | 0 | 0 | 0 | 51 | 0 |
| Union | 0 | 37 | 0 | 2 | 0 | 0 | 0 | 35 | 0 | 0 | 0 | 0 |
| Warren | 82 | 1,019 | 82 | 1,014 | 0 | 0 | 0 | 5 | 0 | 0 | 0 | 0 |
| Washington | 211 | 108 | 118 | 108 | 0 | 0 | 0 | 0 | 0 | 0 | 93 | 0 |
| Wayne | 34 | 2,762 | 34 | 2,336 | 0 | 426 | 0 | 0 | 0 | 0 | 0 | 0 |
| Webster | 62 | 15 | 62 | 15 | 0 | 0 | 0 | 0 | 0 | 0 | 0 | 0 |
| Whitley | 192 | 3,925 | 149 | 2,223 | 0 | 1,301 | 43 | 401 | 0 | 0 | 0 | 0 |
| Wolfe | 171 | 539 | 161 | 539 | 0 | 0 | 5 | 0 | 0 | 0 | 5 | 0 |
| All counties | 11,538 | 174,158 | 4,164 | 140,254 | 7 | 6,538 | 4,187 | 20,420 | 1,929 | 6,946 | 1,251 | 0 |

[a] Includes roundwood delivered to nonpulpmills, then chipped and sold to pulpmills (140,000 cubic feet in 2007).

**Table A.15—Total roundwood output by product, species group, and source of material, Kentucky, 2007**

| Product and species group | All sources | Total | Growing-stock trees | | Other sources |
| | | | Sawtimber | Poletimber | |
| --- | --- | --- | --- | --- | --- |
| | | | *thousand cubic feet* | | |
| **Saw logs** | | | | | |
| Softwood | 4,164 | 4,011 | 3,947 | 64 | 153 |
| Hardwood | 140,254 | 119,405 | 115,251 | 4,154 | 20,849 |
| Total | 144,418 | 123,416 | 119,198 | 4,218 | 21,002 |
| **Veneer logs and bolts** | | | | | |
| Softwood | 7 | 7 | 6 | 0 | 0 |
| Hardwood | 6,538 | 6,311 | 6,138 | 173 | 227 |
| Total | 6,545 | 6,318 | 6,144 | 174 | 227 |
| **Pulpwood** | | | | | |
| Softwood | 4,187 | 3,878 | 2,626 | 1,251 | 309 |
| Hardwood | 20,420 | 18,982 | 6,805 | 12,177 | 1,438 |
| Total | 24,607 | 22,859 | 9,431 | 13,428 | 1,748 |
| **Composite panels** | | | | | |
| Softwood | 1,929 | 1,775 | 1,198 | 577 | 154 |
| Hardwood | 6,946 | 6,565 | 2,354 | 4,211 | 381 |
| Total | 8,875 | 8,340 | 3,552 | 4,788 | 535 |
| **Poles and posts** | | | | | |
| Softwood | 229 | 211 | 168 | 43 | 18 |
| Hardwood | 0 | 0 | 0 | 0 | 0 |
| Total | 229 | 211 | 168 | 43 | 18 |
| **Other miscellaneous** | | | | | |
| Softwood | 1,022 | 940 | 635 | 305 | 82 |
| Hardwood | 0 | 0 | 0 | 0 | 0 |
| Total | 1,022 | 940 | 635 | 305 | 82 |
| **Total industrial products** | | | | | |
| Softwood | 11,538 | 10,822 | 8,580 | 2,241 | 716 |
| Hardwood | 174,158 | 151,263 | 130,548 | 20,715 | 22,895 |
| Total | 185,696 | 162,084 | 139,128 | 22,956 | 23,612 |
| **Domestic fuelwood** | | | | | |
| Softwood | 199 | 151 | 149 | 2 | 48 |
| Hardwood | 20,474 | 18,660 | 18,428 | 231 | 1,814 |
| Total | 20,673 | 18,811 | 18,578 | 234 | 1,862 |
| **All products** | | | | | |
| Softwood | 11,737 | 10,973 | 8,730 | 2,243 | 764 |
| Hardwood | 194,632 | 169,922 | 148,976 | 20,946 | 24,710 |
| Total | 206,369 | 180,895 | 157,706 | 23,189 | 25,474 |

Numbers in rows and columns may not sum to totals due to rounding.

**Table A.16—Total roundwood output by species group, survey region, and ownership class, Kentucky, 2007**

| Species group and survey region | Total | Ownership class | | |
| --- | --- | --- | --- | --- |
| | | Public | Forest industry | Nonindustrial private |
| | | *thousand cubic feet* | | |
| Softwoods | | | | |
| Eastern | 253 | 0 | 8 | 245 |
| Northern Cumberland | 851 | 5 | 0 | 846 |
| Southern Cumberland | 1,730 | 16 | 0 | 1,714 |
| Bluegrass | 1,450 | 18 | 0 | 1,432 |
| Pennyroyal | 1,338 | 6 | 0 | 1,332 |
| Western Coalfield | 3,377 | 0 | 0 | 3,377 |
| Western | 2,738 | 0 | 0 | 2,738 |
| Total softwoods | 11,737 | 45 | 8 | 11,684 |
| Hardwoods | | | | |
| Eastern | 20,193 | 12 | 1,315 | 18,866 |
| Northern Cumberland | 26,271 | 452 | 0 | 25,819 |
| Southern Cumberland | 39,674 | 429 | 0 | 39,245 |
| Bluegrass | 8,734 | 48 | 0 | 8,686 |
| Pennyroyal | 50,587 | 1,010 | 3,969 | 45,607 |
| Western Coalfield | 37,859 | 351 | 0 | 37,508 |
| Western | 11,314 | 854 | 1,250 | 9,210 |
| Total hardwoods | 194,632 | 3,157 | 6,534 | 184,941 |
| All species | 206,369 | 3,201 | 6,542 | 196,625 |

Numbers in rows and columns may not sum to totals due to rounding.

**Table A.17—Total roundwood output by species group, detailed species group, and product, Kentucky, 2007**

| Species group and detailed species group | Total | Saw logs | Veneer logs | Pulpwood | Composite panels | Poles and posts | Other miscellaneous | Domestic fuelwood |
|---|---|---|---|---|---|---|---|---|
| | | | | *thousand cubic feet* | | | | |
| **Softwood** | | | | | | | | |
| Cedar | 181 | 128 | 0 | 1 | 0 | 7 | 42 | 3 |
| Eastern white pine | 142 | 128 | 0 | 1 | 0 | 10 | 0 | 2 |
| Loblolly-shortleaf pine | 603 | 228 | 0 | 218 | 122 | 24 | 0 | 11 |
| Other yellow pines | 10,693 | 3,669 | 7 | 3,966 | 1,701 | 188 | 980 | 182 |
| Hemlock | 118 | 10 | 0 | 0 | 105 | 0 | 0 | 2 |
| Total softwoods | 11,737 | 4,164 | 7 | 4,187 | 1,929 | 229 | 1,022 | 199 |
| **Hardwood** | | | | | | | | |
| Soft maple | 6,888 | 5,323 | 108 | 681 | 52 | 0 | 0 | 725 |
| Hard maple | 5,617 | 3,788 | 113 | 887 | 238 | 0 | 0 | 591 |
| Other birch | 1,372 | 671 | 86 | 391 | 79 | 0 | 0 | 144 |
| Hickory | 21,691 | 15,714 | 778 | 2,079 | 839 | 0 | 0 | 2,281 |
| Beech | 8,098 | 6,088 | 233 | 622 | 304 | 0 | 0 | 852 |
| Ash | 6,083 | 4,593 | 137 | 674 | 39 | 0 | 0 | 640 |
| Black walnut | 2,961 | 2,402 | 86 | 137 | 24 | 0 | 0 | 311 |
| Sweetgum | 4,437 | 3,002 | 39 | 915 | 14 | 0 | 0 | 467 |
| Yellow-poplar | 27,216 | 18,256 | 1,146 | 3,193 | 1,757 | 0 | 0 | 2,863 |
| Blackgum-tupelo | 1,869 | 1,349 | 16 | 247 | 61 | 0 | 0 | 197 |
| Sycamore | 1,195 | 938 | 8 | 98 | 26 | 0 | 0 | 126 |
| Cottonwood | 1,008 | 578 | 44 | 279 | 0 | 0 | 0 | 106 |
| Black cherry | 1,109 | 759 | 45 | 114 | 75 | 0 | 0 | 117 |
| Select white oaks | 27,074 | 21,128 | 1,081 | 1,396 | 622 | 0 | 0 | 2,847 |
| Other white oaks | 13,798 | 9,934 | 652 | 1,305 | 455 | 0 | 0 | 1,451 |
| Select red oaks | 14,734 | 10,262 | 560 | 1,935 | 426 | 0 | 0 | 1,550 |
| Other red oaks | 38,793 | 28,250 | 1,018 | 4,205 | 1,239 | 0 | 0 | 4,081 |
| Basswood | 2,472 | 1,607 | 119 | 226 | 260 | 0 | 0 | 260 |
| Elm | 3,713 | 2,527 | 77 | 659 | 59 | 0 | 0 | 390 |
| Other eastern hardwoods | 4,504 | 3,085 | 191 | 376 | 378 | 0 | 0 | 474 |
| Total hardwoods | 194,632 | 140,254 | 6,538 | 20,420 | 6,946 | 0 | 0 | 20,474 |
| All species | 206,369 | 144,418 | 6,545 | 24,607 | 8,875 | 229 | 1,022 | 20,673 |

Numbers in rows and columns may not sum to totals due to rounding.

**Table A.18—Total roundwood output by species group, detailed species group, and ownership class, Kentucky, 2007**

| Species group and detailed species group | Total | Ownership class | | |
|---|---|---|---|---|
| | | Public | Forest industry | Nonindustrial private |
| | | *thousand cubic feet* | | |
| Softwood | | | | |
| Cedar | 181 | 6 | 0 | 175 |
| Eastern white pine | 142 | 1 | 0 | 140 |
| Loblolly-shortleaf pine | 603 | 6 | 0 | 597 |
| Other yellow pines | 10,693 | 30 | 8 | 10,655 |
| Hemlock | 118 | 1 | 0 | 117 |
| Total softwoods | 11,737 | 45 | 8 | 11,684 |
| Hardwood | | | | |
| Soft maple | 6,888 | 33 | 275 | 6,580 |
| Hard maple | 5,617 | 69 | 654 | 4,894 |
| Other birch | 1,372 | 15 | 0 | 1,357 |
| Hickory | 21,691 | 507 | 461 | 20,723 |
| Beech | 8,098 | 75 | 442 | 7,581 |
| Ash | 6,083 | 118 | 0 | 5,966 |
| Black walnut | 2,961 | 37 | 4 | 2,920 |
| Sweetgum | 4,437 | 179 | 0 | 4,259 |
| Yellow-poplar | 27,216 | 247 | 537 | 26,432 |
| Blackgum-tupelo | 1,869 | 53 | 57 | 1,759 |
| Sycamore | 1,195 | 13 | 0 | 1,182 |
| Cottonwood | 1,008 | 0 | 0 | 1,008 |
| Black cherry | 1,109 | 19 | 43 | 1,046 |
| Select white oaks | 27,074 | 536 | 1,308 | 25,230 |
| Other white oaks | 13,798 | 186 | 885 | 12,727 |
| Select red oaks | 14,734 | 284 | 233 | 14,217 |
| Other red oaks | 38,793 | 615 | 1,349 | 36,828 |
| Basswood | 2,472 | 2 | 154 | 2,316 |
| Elm | 3,713 | 124 | 15 | 3,574 |
| Other eastern hardwoods | 4,504 | 46 | 116 | 4,342 |
| Total hardwoods | 194,632 | 3,157 | 6,534 | 184,941 |
| All species | 206,369 | 3,201 | 6,542 | 196,625 |

Numbers in rows and columns may not sum to totals due to rounding.